poetry in butterfly time

karen kay knauss

Copyright © 2015

In Butterfly Time

Karen Kay Knauss

All Rights Reserved

NO PORTION OF THIS BOOK MAY BE REPRODUCED IN ANY MANNER WHATSOEVER, WITHOUT THE WRITTEN PERMISSION FROM THE COPYRIGHT OWNER, EXCEPT FOR BRIEF EXCERPTS FOR REVIEW PURPOSES.

Artwork: Ian Anderson
Cover Design: Karen Kay Knauss

pTp
peachtreepress@pldi.net
ISBN 9780989592604

Dimensional Consciousness

dare to

      venture beyond tradition
and follow endless horizons

      learn which rules to follow
and which ones to bend

      face the risk of ridicule
and the fear of failure

      taste the sweetness of success
and remain poised through it all

      travel beyond physical existence
to realms of dimensional consciousness

      soar like a butterfly
with illimitable imagination

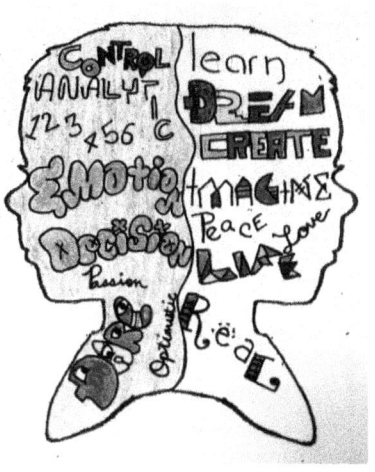

We are not held back by limitations—
fear is what holds us back.

Ian Anderson

*"Logic will take you from A to B.
Imagination will take you everywhere"*

Einstein

Contents

Poems	Page

INVOCATION OF THE MUSES

When Heart Songs Call	4
In Butterfly Time	5
Only If I Choose	6
Snowy Morning	7
In The Stillness	8
Mortality	9
Ephemeral Blush	10
Words	11

AT THE THRESHOLD OF AWARENESS

Threshold of Awareness	16
All That is Ours	17
Things I Left Behind	18
Tiny Things	19
Haiku	20
Haiku	21
Haiku	22
Haiku	23
Haiku	24
Haiku	25
Tanka	26
Tanka	27
Eclipse	28
The Season Ends	29
Where Angels Fly	30

A DIMENSIONAL PERSPECTIVE

In Reflection	33
Hope	34
Praise For Persephone	35
Tenacity	37
The Rest of the Quote	38
Out of the Darkness	39
Circle of Life	40
Despite the Snow	41
Politics and Tricks	42
Easter Sunday	43
I Am Only a Child	45
I Believe	46
Tedium	47
To Begin Again	48
Hidden Things	49
Like Hummingbirds and Butterflies	50

DANCING IN MY RED SHOES

A Voice So Clear	54
With Poetry	55
The Newness of the Day	56
The Sweetest Store	57
Know Our Names	58
Quiet Days	59
How I Love You	60
Kissed by the Oklahoma Wind	61
More Than Dreams	62
Like Snowflakes	63
Dreams	64
And I Have Seen—	66

The Wide Window	70
Butterflies and Endless Days	72
Return of the Butterfly	74
Author Bio	76
Body of Works	78

The Wide Window

I want to ride
>> this train
>>>> and sit by the window,

the wide window
>> that opens up
>>>> and consumes me,

not stranded
>> on the isle
>>>> of certain ennui,

not restrained
>> by opinions
>>>> on either side,

not buried
>> beneath words
>>>> that overwhelm

>>>>>> my own.

Ian Anderson

soaring on wings of a butterfly

Invocation of the Muses

When Heart Songs Call

When piercingly they call
      from recesses
           deep within—

I answer with Athena.
She lifts the mortal veil
that covers the eyes,
hardens the heart,
and silences the soul.
With unrestrained passion,
we transcend the physical
we enter the illimitable
realms of imagination
we fly on the wings of words
that sing the poet's song.
She opens my eyes,
softens my heart,
speaks to my soul—

I pen the poetry
      of endless
           heart songs.

In Butterfly Time

In the brevity of seasons
    they flutter and frolic about
        like carefree children at play.

Vivid orange wings catch my eye
    as they dart from lilies to lilacs,
        sipping up the sweet nectar of life.

Seemingly, they give little
    thought to measured time
        by One so divinely planned.

With captivating presence
    they stir a sense of serenity,
        even as winter's chill impends.

To high Sierras they must
    fly and cling to precious life,
        soon to be given for another.

I would be like a soft-winged
    butterfly— soaring serenely
        in the warmth and brevity of life.

Only if I Choose

Yet for faith,
Would I shrink in fear
For strength,
Would I hesitate and fall,
For truth,
Would I blame and fail.

Do I fear
Because *others* have doubted my faith?
Do I fall
Because *others* have broken my will?
Do I fail
Because *others* have been to blame?

I fear
Only if I choose despair.
I fall,
Only if I choose weakness.
I fail,
Only if I choose deception.

Snowy Morning

The splendor of Dawn
will not be seen
on the vanishing horizon,
the snow-laden cedars,
frozen lakes, or white dusted fields.
Emily's "Celestial Vail"
has been drawn in the night.

Although
a tepid pink
pervades the gloomy gray—
a distant presence
will not be denied.

Behind the silver clouds
her fiery chariot
races on into another's view—
hurling the glorious news
of this December day.

In The Stillness

The stillness of this morning
is interrupted by fox squirrels
scampering across the yard
up the tree,
and into densely woven dreys
for warmth and nutty cache

by flurries of hungry birds
swooping down upon the deck
cautiously,
with nervous jerks and gestures
they bend and peck and nibble
bend and peck and nibble.

This snowy morning
is like a silent movie
noiseless—
yet busy with unfolding life.

Mortality

sometime
during a heavy
starless night—
eyes close unaware

falls latticed crystals
quietly to their place
upon the earth—
one by one
remarkably rare

inevitably
to be forgotten—
lost in the multitude

disappearing helplessly
in gusting winds
dispelling rain
or softening sun

Ephemeral Blush

I saw the face of Dawn
she blushed in pink

it reflected
onto her flowing hair
her hands and fingers
the waking pond
the dry winter grass

a blushing backdrop
for bare-branched trees—
she took my breath away

for a moment

Words

There are some who say
all that I see and hear
smell, touch and taste—
all that I sense
need not be written
with words.

Still,
I feel compelled to share

what the four winds speak to me
as they whisper of the seasons
or bellow of the storms

why the birds seem to sing
their simple songs for me—
and sometimes
even to mourn for me

where the winding river runs
as it leads me on this journey—
what to carry, what to leave behind

how the sea pulls me
out into a vast awareness
then lets me rush back
in waves of sensation.

If words linger
after the book is closed—

then I have shared
with those to whom
I shall never speak.

At the Threshold of Awareness

Threshold of Awareness

I will not rest
in the confines of a tomb
with my cold clay vessel

You will find me running with the summer wind.

my heart song
has no funerary verse—
its joyful chorus echoes

You will hear its melody across the red bed plains.

my spirit will transcend
the limitations of mortality
to unknown realms of awareness

You will see me soaring like a butterfly.

All That is Ours

We are always in one moment,
One moment from the past,
    How quickly may be taken
    All that was ours to embrace.

We are always in one moment,
One moment from the future,
    How quickly we are given
    All that will be ours to embrace.

We are always in one moment,
One moment from the past,
One moment from the future.

    How quickly we must seize
    All that is ours to embrace.

Things I Left Behind

I left dishes in the sink
dust where it had settled
floors with usual tracks.

I left hair undone
nails unpolished, ears unadorned
face au naturel.

I left movies, luncheons
concerts, art festivals in the park
the droning six o'clock news.

I left wardrobe to casual chance
piles of fallen leaves to the wind,
worries to be driven by destiny.

I left inhibitions and fears of ridicule
I wore Dorothy's red shoes
I soared with imaginary wings.

Tiny Things

A tiny seed—
If planted
And nurtured every day
Will become
A mighty tree.

A tiny dream—
If imagined
And nurtured every day
Will become
A mighty reality.

rising columns spin
black rain, wild wind, earth's debris—
death dance in spring sky

splendid blooms open
sweet fragrances fill cool air—
welcome Ides of Spring

red-tailed hawk circles
bighorn sheep cling to rift wall
Rio Grande runs wild

autumn's aged leaves
cold winds carry far away—
butterflies return

weep not mighty ones
for loss of resplendent leaves—
splendid silhouettes

golden Aspen leaves
drift with long brown pine needles
weaving winter's throw

October harvest
red chili ristras strung tight—
sunshine leaves early

cold river runs low
golden cottonwoods shiver—
rise October sun

swirling north winds lift
red and golden leaves in waltz—
applaud Mother Earth

north winds carry chill
red apples fall from tired trees—
sweet winter savor

winds of November
stir yesterday memories—
asleep, never dead

December lies down
breathes beneath blankets of snow—
brief quiescent sleep

turn the new year page
mark another chapter end—
December and I

charcoal filigree
silhouette rosy canvas—
ephemeral joy

her spirit within
the binding blemish of birth
sweet death will set free

scattered near and far
no thought of where they may fall—
careless evil words

somnolent gray eyes
stare with steeped nihility—
sad society

Tanka

golden leaves flutter
making music with north winds
across san juan slopes
rocking the ancient valley
with their aspen lullaby

Tanka

magpie in aspen
strident chirps on chilling breeze
I rush to answer—
take flight to faraway home
magpie waits in red cedar

Eclipse

My sorrow is like
a heavy black shadow that
covers
  my
    soul—
I see no hope for the
future, I remember
no joy from
  the
    past.

The Season Ends

as the asters wilt and shed
their tired, purple petals—
as golden leaves from
birch and cottonwoods
drift and curl into sleep—
as clear fountain waters
chill and thicken in autumn air—
as six, chirping magpies
fly away together

Where Angels Fly

The *nameless one*
came and led me to a desert
where the crescent moon
transcended into a golden lake

where sand dunes
sing softly in the wind,
and the tea and horse road
lies beneath silk—

somewhere
in that far away place
of pithy wisdom.

A Dimensional Perspective

In Reflection

My songs are many,
though none the same

hushed not and timeless,
their notes still clear

and oft-resounding
life's marked refrains.

Hope

On a bare-branched morning
With not much color in the sky
There is only one
        Little black bird
                In the feeder.

Still—
There is a hint of pink light
Breaking on the horizon.

Praise for Persephone

I noticed
tender shoots eagerly emerging
from wild sand plum roots
as the earth began to warm.

Soon the thickets
would be frilly white bouquets
scattered along sandy roads
or rising up out of a sea
of green grass.

The pendulum of time
began to swing
as I fell into nostalgic dreams
where childhood memories
emerged as well.

We gave no thought
to winged pest
we shooed away,
or for the sense
of buzzing swarms.

We shuffled barefoot
through the countless tracks
of awakened creatures
that sheltered within
the thicket's maze.

We celebrated the season
beneath that fragrant canopy—
unaware of those who
offered up ancient prayers
to Persephone.

Tenacity

The north wind is fierce
fluffed-up coats with
red-tipped tails and tuffs
bend toward the south.

With a sense of urgency
they peck at swirling seeds—

both
refusing to blow away.

The Rest of the Quote

There but for the grace of God go I

There but for good parents go I
There but for an education go I
There but for hard work go I
There but for circumstance go I

Out of the Darkness

When the stars shine
On Oklahoma again—

We will find courage
To look up and go on.

Homes may be lost
Hearts may be broken
Lives may be taken—

We have been in the
Heaven's darkness before.

The stars will shine again—
Always within our reach.

Circle of Life

In spite of fears of the unknown,
Give me strength to be born.

In spite of youthful bliss,
Give me inspiration to press on.

In spite of dreams fulfilled,
Give me meekness of heart.

In spite of life's injustice,
Give me freedom from blame.

In spite of darkened days,
Give me enduring assurance.

In spite of fears of the unknown,
Give me peace to die.

Despite the Snow

The grayness
of this snowy morning
was awakened
with a tint of rose
hanging on the horizon—
as quickly as it fell
upon the icy lake
it faded away.

Yet
russet leaves
orange persimmons
red, blue, and green berries
refused to leave
their lacey branches bare—
colorless and cold.

Politics and Tricks

Let's play that old game with a trick,
Let's spin even if we get sick.
For votes, we can lie,
The truth, just deny,
For sure with our gold we can trick!

Easter Sunday

I was interrupted
by memories—

watching
my mother
take the final stitch
on a pink chiffon dress

waiting
for my father's
nod of approval

waving
at grandparents
passing by slowly—
a subtle reminder
that all the good seats
will surely be taken

sitting
in that small town
Church of Christ
with family and friends
hymnals, bulletins
hard paper fans
hard wooden chairs

listening
to the sermon
about Gethsemane—
when all I understood
about gardens
was golden Daffodils
blooming in ours

thinking
that death was simply
an incomprehensible
word to me

I paused—
I gave in to the Easter
morning interruptions,
put the inconsequential
schedule and fretting aside,
and with my memories—
I became a child again.

I Am Only a Child

Don't tell me how,
Show me.

Don't tell me no,
Teach me.

Don't tell me I'm bad,
Forgive me.

Don't tell me I'm lost,
Lead me.

I Believe.....

I do not need a Sabbath Day
to worship,
Nor sanction from a clergyman.
I do not need a congregation
to pray,
Or lofty choir to sing.
I do not need
to be understood.

I simply need this day
to offer praise,
And for His favor humbly plead.
I simply need the voice within
to call His name,
Or chime with Nature's song.
I simply
need to be.

Tedium

For one who has no vision,

The future will be the same as the past,

And for all one's tedious toils—

Today will never matter!

To Begin Again

The evening is cool
and free of care

prairie stars
twinkle in delight

calliope music
fills the autumn air

and carousels
go round and round

pausing—
only to begin again.

Hidden Things

The dense fog
creeps in and settles
over the land.

Familiar trees and lake
even the brightest of stars
vanish before my eyes—

like wintering monarchs
with closed, gray wings
in the oyamel forests

like the great heron
in reedy shallows
of blue-gray waters

like the coyote
in a snow dusted field
of coppery brown grass

there—
hidden somewhere.

Like Hummingbirds and Butterflies

The needled carpet
laid by pines
was soft with sound
beneath my feet,
they carried me
in sweet pursuit
with hummingbirds
and butterflies.

I walked
upon the mountain side
to find the lovely columbines,
they grow and bloom
wherever they please—

without a bed
or garden row.

Dancing in My Red Shoes

A Voice So Clear

When from the heart
And recesses deep within
Peal the voiceless thoughts
By one who pens,

There is no voice so clear
As piercingly they call

And echo
Through the years.

With Poetry

Dancing out of my sadness

   out of my silence

      out of my shadow

         Dancing in my red shoes

The Newness of the Day

I hear the rumbling
of a yellow bus,
it slows
for designated stops.

I see the children
waiting there,
bright-eyed
shouldering
homework-stuffed
backpacks.

I think
about another day,
another time—

I sense the newness
of the day,
what will we
learn along its way?

The Sweetest Store

Hurry now,
The winds blow cold.

Gather fruit
beneath the trees
and gently wrap
with papers thin.
Round the wooden
baskets full
and cellar
in the hollow ground.

Savor then
the sweetest store,
when sleeping trees
are wintry bare.

Know Our Names

Pages rare
to us revealed.
Voices faint,
yet unrestrained,
Steal upon
our listening ear,
Now affirm
their time
long passed.

Still resounds
their message clear,
Know our names—
in you we live.

Quiet Days

I watched her sewing there,
Loading the spool pin with thread
Squinting her eyes to see the eye
Winding the silver bobbin
That locked in every perfect stitch.

Her feet pushed the rocking treadle
With toe and heel, the same way
She pushed the rocking chair—
Toe and heel, toe and heel,
Until I fell asleep.

How I Love You

Like the sunrise
brings the morning light
as it gently leaves
the dark of night

like the quiet
summer rain
as it falls upon
the windowpane

like the sunset
on a restful sea
as it lingers there
for you and me.

Kissed by the Oklahoma Wind

Within ancient places
Beats the heart of red lands,

Home and hunting grounds
Of nomadic natives.

Above Red Bed Plains,
Tall Grass Prairies,

Cowboy Flats and
The Cimarron Breaks,

Scissortail dance
In daring descent.

Over Southern Plains
And Indian Grass prairies.

Oklahoma winds welcome
Their April return

While Indian Blankets
Bloom near low rolling hills.

More Than Dreams

Inspiration!
It is only
A motivation taken in—
With little effort.

Inspiration!
It is only
A reality when given back—
With great effort.

Like Snowflakes

Sometime
during the heavy
starless night
bare branched trees
lost their shadows,

latticed crystals fell
quietly to their place
upon the earth—
one by one
remarkably unique.

Inevitability
and soon
to be forgotten—

disappearing helplessly
in gusting winds
dispelling rain
or softening sun.

Remembered—
if only an impression
revisited in the words
of a simple poem.

Dreams

The ones that came true

The ones that did not

The ones that are still waiting

And I have seen—

in early November
gathering apples
for winter storage,
twelve trumpeter swans
soaring in precise formation
through low-hanging clouds
at an amazing speed.

With outstretched necks
and flared white wings
they landed gracefully
upon the millpond
with huge black-webbed feet.

The swans
settled into the water effortlessly,
kinked their long necks back
and rested in grandeur—
as certain
of their destination
as monarchs in spring,
as natural as bees
returning to the hive.

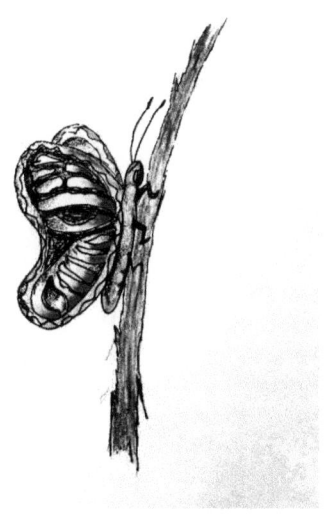

*We cannot allow fear of the unknown
to hold us back from our full potential.*

Ian Anderson

The Wide Window

I want to ride
    this train
        and sit by the window,

the wide window
    that opens up
        and consumes me,

not stranded
    on the isle
        of certain ennui,

not restrained
    by opinions
        on either side,

not buried
    beneath words
        that overwhelm

            my own.

Butterflies and Endless Days

Each day
I watch them—

soon
they will fly
away on soft wings
and disappear into
an endless sky

fly away
before my eyes,
like days gone by
on wings of time

days
I thought were mine—
and endless.

Return of the Butterfly

They flutter
in the warmth of light,

then autumn flight
takes them to where
cold winds are rare—

where dew sustains
in mountains high
until spring draws nigh.

By garden's gate
pink phlox await

as I
before the windowsill.

When winter's chill
is no concern—

they will return.

Karen Kay Knauss

Karen grew up in Caddo County on a small farm where her family managed a large fruit orchard. She studied at the University of Science and Arts of Oklahoma and earned a Bachelor of Arts. She has enjoyed careers in music, teaching, and fine art. Her unique hand cast fiber sculptures hang in public and private collections across the United States and in several foreign countries, and she performs in the vocal duo, Heart & Soul.

Karen has authored two chapbooks and five poetry collections, including a historical collection of poems about Oklahoma. She has co-authored two genealogical chronicles, and presents readings and lectures for special events at universities, libraries, and museums. She has received numerous awards for her poetry in statewide, regional, and national competitions.

Karen is a member of several State Poetry Societies and serves as the Treasurer for the Poetry Society of Oklahoma. She was awarded Poet Laureate by the Society, and was nominated as Oklahoma State Poet Laureate.

works by Karen Kay Knauss

Poetry Collections

OKLAHOMA COAL FIRES

The Thorny Truth and Their Civil War

77 Pieces of Poetry About Oklahoma

A Gathering of Pearls

In Butterfly Time

Poetry Chapbooks

Deep Blue Waters

Leaving Flatland by Poetry

Genealogical Chronicles
Co-Author, Kathleen Knauss McCullar

KNAUSS FAMILY HISTORY
TRULL FAMILY HISTORY

PTP
peachtreepress@pldi.net
2015